The World of Martial Arts
Kung Fu

By Jim Ollhoff

Published by ABDO Publishing Company, 8000 West 78th Street, Suite 310, Edina, MN 55439.
Copyright ©2008 by Abdo Consulting Group, Inc. International copyrights reserved in all countries.
No part of this book may be reproduced in any form without written permission from the publisher.
ABDO & Daughters™ is a trademark and logo of ABDO Publishing Company.

Printed in the United States.

Editor: John Hamilton
Graphic Design: John Hamilton
Cover Design: Neil Klinepier
Cover Illustration: Corbis
Interior Photos and Illustrations: p 1 kung fu stylists sparring, Getty Images; p 5 three Chinese monks sparring, Corbis; p 7 monk stretching leg, Corbis; p 9 monk kicking, Getty Images; p 10 map of China, Getty Images; p 11 (upper left) elderly monk, Corbis; p 11 (upper right) Bodhidharma; p 12 painting of monks practicing kung fu, Corbis; p 13 woman demonstrating kung fu ready stance, iStockphoto; p 15 motion-blur of monks sparring, iStockphoto; p 16 (top) dragon, iStockphoto; p 16 (center) snake, iStockphoto; p 16 (bottom) tiger, iStockphoto; p 17 (upper left) crane, iStockphoto; p 17 (upper right) leopard, iStockphoto; p 17 (bottom) kung fu stylist, iStockphoto; p 18 man performs side kick, Getty Images; p 19 ready stance, Getty Images; p 20 self-defense demonstration, Corbis; p 21 kung fu class, Getty Images; p 23 front punch, Getty Images; p 24 white crane kung fu, Getty Images; p 25 group performing tai chi, Getty Images; p 27 mantis stance, Corbis; p 28 Bruce Lee, Getty Images; p 29 Jackie Chan on cover of TIME, Getty Images; p 31 man performing tai chi in meadow, iStockphoto.

Library of Congress Cataloging-in-Publication Data

Ollhoff, Jim, 1959-
    Kung fu / Jim Ollhoff.
        p. cm. -- (The world of martial arts)
    Includes index.
    ISBN 978-1-59928-978-6
    1. Kung fu--Juvenile literature. I. Title.

GV1114.7.O55 2008
796.8159--dc22
                                2007030548

CONTENTS

Centuries Ago in China...

Centuries ago in China, an old man walked along a forest path. As he rounded a corner, he saw three bandits attacking a farmer. The old man proceeded toward them, leaning on his cane as he walked. In a voice that was firm and soft, he said, "Leave that man alone."

"Be on your way," commanded one of the bandits. He was a huge man, tall and muscular. "Go away!"

The frail old man replied calmly, "When you do evil, only evil comes back to you."

The bandit grew angry. He kicked a tree trunk, breaking it in half. "Stop preaching, old man, or I'll smash you like I did this tree!"

"You do not frighten me," replied the old man, in the same calm voice.

The bandit lost his temper completely. He shouted and tried to kick the old man. But the old man, with only a small movement of his arm, gracefully caught the bandit's leg and pushed it slightly. The bandit lost his balance and crashed to the ground on his back.

The second bandit, a tall woman, drew her sword and slashed at the old man's head. However, he moved ever so slightly and dodged away from the sword. The momentum of the woman's sword made her lose balance. The old man darted in and pushed her, causing her to fall to her knees.

The third bandit leaped for the old man's legs, but the old man grabbed the bandit's chin. The old man spun around and threw the third bandit head first into a pool of mud. All three bandits got up, outraged at their treatment, and all attacked the old man at the same time. Suddenly, they all found themselves in a pile by the side of the path. The old man stood calmly, completely unharmed.

The bandits suddenly realized they were in the presence of a great kung fu master from the Shaolin Temple. He and others from China created a system of defensive fighting known as *kung fu*. The bandits fell to their knees, apologized, and begged the old man to teach them his skills. "I cannot teach you my fighting art," said the kung fu master. "The martial arts are only for those who are good of character, and will protect others from people like you. You are the type of people who would never understand my teachings."

Above: Three Chinese monks practice kung fu, with two monks attacking the third.

Kung Fu Terms

The martial arts that come from China are called by many different names, and spelled many different ways. In the United States, the most common term for the Chinese martial arts is kung fu. In the Chinese language, kung fu means "achievement through great effort." To become good at the martial arts is a great achievement, but it only comes through great effort, and many years of practice. Sometimes kung fu is spelled and pronounced *gongfu*, or *gung fu*.

The term kung fu was not used until the 20th century, even though Chinese martial arts are hundreds, perhaps thousands, of years old. Technically, the Chinese term kung fu can refer to the achievement of any skill that requires great effort and long, hard work. Therefore, someone can be a carpenter, or an artist, with great kung fu.

When Americans and Europeans first saw kung fu in China, they called it *Chinese boxing*. They knew and understood the sport of boxing, and it was the closest comparison they could make.

Sometimes authors of martial arts books use the term *chuan fa*, which means "way of the fist." Other authors use the term *Shaolin martial arts*, or *Shaolin kung fu*. Much of what we see in the martial arts was created, perfected, and kept alive in the Shaolin Buddhist Temple. In China, the official term for martial arts is *wu shu*, which means "martial art." This book will use the term *kung fu*, which is the name most often used in the United States.

Facing page:
A Shaolin Buddhist monk from China demonstrates the extreme flexibility that years of kung fu training can accomplish.

The Origins of Kung Fu

Facing page: A monk from the Shaolin Temple in Dengfeng, Henan Province, China, shows off his kung fu kicking ability. Many people say that the Shaolin Temple is the birthplace of kung fu.

China is often called the "birthplace of martial arts." However, identifying the exact history is difficult. Paintings of people wrestling, fighting, and carrying weapons have been unearthed in Egypt that date from 2500 B.C. Does this mean the martial arts started in Egypt? Or did Chinese masters teach martial arts to those in Egypt? Or does it mean that Chinese martial artists existed in 2500 B.C., but didn't leave any written documents or paintings? Historians don't know the answer.

It appears that China was the first to connect martial arts to religious philosophy, and the first to create a series of schools of martial arts. The Chinese also appear to be the first to make the martial arts practical for self-defense. Together, these facts point to the Chinese as creators of the first martial arts system.

The Chinese began kung fu, but it is impossible to say how kung fu began. Kung fu masters for hundreds of years kept their art a strict secret. Students were often forbidden from telling anyone they were practicing martial arts. This secrecy, plus kung fu's long history—at least 1,500 years— makes it difficult to say how the martial arts began.

There is one popular legend that says an Indian monk named Bodhidharma started kung fu. (In Chinese, his name is Tamo). In approximately the year 500 A.D., a Buddhist monk named Bodhidharma left India. He walked for many months, through forests, swamps, and over mountains, and finally arrived in China. He traveled to a Buddhist temple in central China. This temple was tucked away in a green forest, and was called *Shaolin,* which means "young forest." According to this legend, Bodhidharma taught the monks at the Shaolin Temple about Zen, a type of meditation that requires sitting for a long time.

Bodhidharma tried to teach the students about Zen, but they were not physically fit. They were inactive, obese, and out of shape. They tried to meditate, but frequently fell asleep when they sat too long. They were so unhealthy that Bodhidharma knew they could never learn anything until they became stronger and healthier. He knew he had to teach them how to exercise.

Below: A map of modern China and surrounding countries.

Above: A portrait of Bodhidharma, the possible founder of the martial art of kung fu.
Left: An elderly monk at China's Shaolin Temple.

Bodhidharma watched how animals moved. He knew that animals were physically fit, so he decided that he could create exercises that were similar to animal "exercises." He copied animal movements and created a series of exercises for humans. He taught the monks how to move like a tiger, a monkey, a crane, or a praying mantis. The monks practiced these movements and became physically fit. Not only that, but Bodhidharma realized that when the monks were attacked by bandits, the monks knew how to defend themselves. They were using the same movements that animals used to defend themselves.

As the years went on, the Shaolin monks refined their techniques. Their fighting style became more and more effective. They refined their fighting methods but continued to copy animal movements. Even today, many styles of kung fu are named after animals. Individual movements have animal names as well, like "the lion chases its tail," or "eagle spreads its wings."

The idea that Bodhidharma created the martial arts is a popular story, but it probably isn't completely true. Historians disagree about many parts of Bodhidharma's life. The idea that he created the martial arts was first written down in a story that is only a few hundred years old, more than 1,000 years after Bodhidharma came to China. It is almost certainly a mix of folklore and fiction, with only a sprinkling of fact.

Below: A centuries-old painting of two Shaolin monks practicing kung fu.

There are other stories about the origin of kung fu in China. One story is about a 13-year-old girl named Shuen Guan, who was born in about 265 A.D. She could fight so well that her nickname was "Little Tigress." A large group of bandits attacked her town. She fought bravely against the bandits, then escaped to a neighboring village where there was a military camp. She talked to the general. He was so impressed with her that he sent his soldiers to help the town. The soldiers, together with Shuen Guan, fought off the bandits, who never returned.

Historians don't know exactly how kung fu started. However, they know how kung fu grew. The Shaolin Temple nurtured the growth of kung fu. Buddhist monks practiced kung fu and refined it over the centuries, making it better and better.

Below: A woman demonstrates a kung fu fighting stance.

Kung Fu's Uniqueness

Kung fu has some distinct differences compared to other martial arts. Generally, kung fu emphasizes speed over power. This is not true for every single Chinese style or technique, but it is a general, overall philosophy. For example, a person who studies Okinawan karate prefers to develop one strong punch that can knock a person out. On the other hand, a kung fu stylist might prefer six punches delivered one right after the other before an attacker can respond. The kung fu strikes may not be as powerful as the karate punch, but they are much faster.

Another kung fu preference is getting in close to an opponent. Karate stylists keep a short distance away from attackers so they can launch hard kicks and punches. Most kung fu stylists like to move in close and deliver short, quick strikes.

Another common kung fu technique is the use of circular movements, instead of straight, linear movements. If an attacker throws a punch, the karate stylist might execute an upblock—a straight movement to push the punch off to the side. A kung fu stylist, on the other hand, might execute a circular block. In a circular block, the fist makes a circle before it blocks the attacker's punch. This sets up the next move, possibly trapping the arm or moving in for an elbow or punch.

Kung fu is different from other martial arts. However, there are also many different styles of kung fu. Each have different ways of teaching, different ways of movement, and different techniques. There are hundreds of styles of kung fu. Some are very popular, while others are only practiced by a few people.

Above: Kung fu stylists perform a sword routine. Kung fu is known for its fast, circular motions.

The Five Animals of Kung Fu

Dragon

Many of the techniques of kung fu are named after animals. The early Shaolin monks admired the characteristics of certain animals for both martial arts as well as life. They admired the agility of the monkey, and the stability of the elephant. While many animals appear in kung fu, five are most important: the dragon, tiger, snake, leopard, and crane.

Snake

In Chinese mythology, the dragon is powerful and gracefully majestic. Dragon movements are graceful and flowing. A dragon-style kung fu master could easily evade a punch by shifting his or her body quickly without stepping aside.

A snake movement is fast and sleek. A snake-style movement would be to coil around an attacker's punch and then strike the arm or other vulnerable point.

A tiger moves with awesome power, but also surprising agility. Tiger movements strike with open hands, and may bend forward to strike powerfully.

Tiger

Crane

Leopard

A leopard movement is very fast and deadly. It strikes with a flat fist, with fingers bent at the second knuckle instead of the third knuckle, like a traditional fist.

The crane lifts its wings elegantly, but delivers forceful blows. A crane movement may strike from high up, with the fingertips. Another crane movement is to extend the knuckle of one's index finger, which is called the phoenix eye.

Kung fu stylist

Advanced kung fu stylists use all movements in combinations. They block with one animal movement and strike with another. The kung fu stylist uses a combination of blinding speed and bone-crushing power. The combinations depend on how the martial artist wishes to subdue an attacker.

HARD AND SOFT STYLE KUNG FU

O ne traditional way to organize the Chinese martial arts is by describing them as hard or soft styles. Hard martial arts, sometimes called external martial arts, began in the southern parts of China. These styles are often associated with the Shaolin Temple in China. The idea of the hard styles is that force must be met with force. So, if an attacker is coming at you, you respond by going at them just as hard, or harder. If an attacker throws a punch, you block it with an equal amount of force. In hard-style kung fu, you use straight punches and kicks to defeat attackers. Some common hard styles of kung fu include *hung gar, wing chun,* and *white crane.*

Facing page: A kung fu hard stylist prepares to practice his form. *Right:* Hard-style kung fu responds to an attack with an equal amount of force, such as this side kick.

The soft styles, or internal martial arts, come mainly from the northern parts of China. The soft styles are just as effective as the hard styles, but have a different philosophy. In the soft styles, you never meet incoming force with equal force. Instead, you use an attacker's own weight and momentum against him or her. So, if someone charges forward, you step off to the side. Then you grab the attacker's arm and pull forward, causing him or her to lose balance and fall to the ground. If someone grabs you, you step back so they have to follow you, and then you switch directions so they are off balance. In soft-style kung fu, martial artists are always moving their feet, switching directions, and keeping attackers off balance. Some popular soft styles include *pa-kua, tai chi chuan, praying mantis, eagle claw,* and *monkey.*

Below: A kung fu self-defense demonstration in Shanghai, China.

The difference between hard styles and soft styles may no longer be very important. Almost all styles today have a mixture of hard and soft techniques. Also, some instructors define hard and soft in different ways, so it is even difficult to get agreement on what these terms mean.

Another confusing fact is that some techniques have the same name as a style. A technique is a thing you do—a punch, kick, or defense against a grab. So, for some people, monkey style is a technique, but for others it is an actual kung fu style.

Above: Most styles of kung fu practiced today use a mix of soft and hard techniques.

POPULAR STYLES OF KUNG FU

HUNG GAR

This Shaolin style of kung fu was developed by Hung Hei Gune, who developed it after studying a style called *tiger fist*. Hung gar makes use of wide, powerful stances. The feet don't move as much as in other styles, but the strikes and blocks are very powerful. Hung gar also teaches a strong philosophy of self-control and respecting others. Hung gar stylists use many weapons, but their favorite is the tiger fork, which has a long handle and a three-pronged fork on the end.

WING CHUN

Facing page: Both hung gar and wing chun styles use powerful stances and quick attacks along a straight line. In wing chun, especially, there is very little wasted motion before a strike.

Wing chun is famous because it is the style in which film star Bruce Lee trained. Bruce Lee later started his own style. Bruce Lee's wing chun teacher was a famous instructor named Yip Man. Wing chun, according to legend, was started by a woman named Yim Wing Chun, who was the only survivor of an attack on a Buddhist temple. She developed a style that emphasized fast, short movements rather than brute strength. Wing chun stylists have very little wasted movement. There are no fancy, decorative moves in wing chun. It consists of short, direct, fast movements that get the job done.

Above: White crane kung fu may have originated in Tibet or western China.

WHITE CRANE

White crane kung fu may have originated in Tibet or western China, and then was taught in the kung fu schools of southern China. White crane movements in many ways resemble a crane, with wide wings and a dangerous beak. Hand strikes often begin from high above the head and then drop down with devastating power. Sometimes, one hand confuses an attacker while the other hand strikes. White crane stylists make use of circling motions to keep attackers off balance.

PA-KUA

Pa-kua kung fu, sometimes spelled *pa kwa* or *bakwa*, teaches eight different angles for attacks. It is a northern soft style, so the pa-kua stylist is less interested in hard, direct punches. In fact, 90 percent of the techniques of pa-kua use an open hand. The pa-kua stylist is always moving, so there is no need to learn strong stances. When an attacker lunges, the pa-kua stylist will move quickly to the side of the attacker, and deliver devastating strikes or throws.

武 道

Left: A group of people perform a tai chi form in a public square in Shanghai, China.

TAI CHI CHUAN

Tai chi chuan, sometimes shortened to *tai chi*, is a martial art that uses soft, flowing movements, usually in slow motion. Some people don't think of tai chi as a martial art, but rather as an exercise, like yoga. In fact, in China, it is common to see people out in the park at dawn, practicing the graceful movements of tai chi. One legend says that a Taoist priest created tai chi several hundred years ago after watching a snake and bird fighting. He copied the movements to create a martial art that uses grace instead of brute force.

Praying Mantis

A Chinese man named Wang Lang created praying mantis style many hundreds of years ago. While he sat resting, after having been beaten in a fight, he watched as a praying mantis insect battled and won against a much larger insect. The praying mantis has strong legs and a vice-like grip, and that's what praying mantis stylists practice to achieve. The hands are bent, like a praying mantis. Martial artists who use this style step forward and deliver quick, powerful strikes.

Eagle Claw

According to legend, this style was copied from the movements of an eagle almost 1,000 years ago. An eagle uses a deadly combination of speed, strength, and cleverness to attack its prey. Eagle claw stylists use these same traits. This style teaches that there are 108 pressure points on the human body. When eagle claw stylists learn how to apply pressure to these points, they have a great advantage over attackers.

Monkey Style

One of the most unusual styles of kung fu began, according to legend, by watching how monkeys fight. Monkey stylists are very deceptive, with many stances that are crouched low to the floor. They roll and tumble, but then spring up to strike powerfully. Perhaps the most unusual variation is *drunken monkey kung fu*. The drunken monkey stylist will pretend to be drunk, swaying and stepping from side to side. The monkey style is difficult to learn, but it is very effective.

Above: A woman practices kung fu in a public square in Taipei, Taiwan. Her feet are in a cat stance, and her hands and arms are in a position that resembles a praying mantis. Mantis stylists deliver quick, powerful strikes with their bent wrists. The style is also useful for hooking an opponent's arms and legs.

KUNG FU COMES TO AMERICA

The first kung fu school outside of China opened in Hawaii in 1922. But most Americans hadn't heard of kung fu until the late 1960s, when a little-known actor named Bruce Lee appeared in a TV series called *The Green Hornet*. Lee played the part of Kato, the driver of a masked crime fighter. Bruce Lee was able to show off his remarkable speed and fighting style in this show.

Bruce Lee went on to be a guest on a number of TV shows. He made a few movies that were released in the

Right: Bruce Lee in a scene from *Enter the Dragon.*

United States (although he had made other movies in China). His speed, strength, and sense of humor instantly made him famous. However, in 1973, during the filming of a movie, he tragically died from an allergy to a medicine.

While Bruce Lee made the fighting style of kung fu famous, another popular TV series highlighted the martial art's Shaolin roots. The TV show was *Kung Fu*, starring David Carradine, which aired from 1972 to 1975. The show was set in the late 1800s. It was about a Shaolin priest who left China looking for his half-brother in the American West. It showed the fighting style of kung fu, but also showed how religion and Chinese philosophy were also a part of the unique fighting style.

Above: The cover of the October 15, 1998, issue of TIME Asia, featuring Jackie Chan.

Chinese actor Jackie Chan also helped popularize kung fu with a number of movies made in Asia and the United States. Jackie Chan's movies usually contain a lot of comedy. The films highlight his superior fighting style and make people laugh at the same time.

Chinese Buddhist monks have also traveled throughout the world, making kung fu more popular. These monks perform incredible feats of strength and graceful finesse, showing what kung fu can do for a student. Today, kung fu schools are popular throughout the United States and all over the world.

GLOSSARY

Buddhism

Buddhism is often called a religion, but it is also referred to as a philosophy, a path to lead an ethical life. Buddhists study the teachings of Siddhartha Gautama, a prince born in today's Nepal who abandoned his former life and roamed northeastern India in the 5th century, seeking enlightenment and the meaning of life. After attaining great wisdom, he became known as Gautama Buddha, or "the Awakened One." The great majority of Buddhists today live in Asia, including China, the likely birthplace of kung fu.

Gongfu

Another word for kung fu.

Kung Fu

A Chinese martial art that had an early influence on the development of other martial arts worldwide, such as karate. The phrase kung fu means "achievement through great effort."

Monk

A person who lives in a religious community. Monks usually take certain vows, such as nonviolence or poverty, to help them focus less on the distractions of the outside world. Buddhist monks from China's Shaolin Temple were some of the first to use kung fu, both as a method of exercise and self-defense, and as a way to clear the mind.

Okinawa

The birthplace of modern karate. The main island of Okinawa is part of the Ryukyu chain of islands, which are situated in the Pacific Ocean south of Japan. Although it was once an independent nation, Okinawa today is a prefecture, or state, of Japan.

Shaolin Temple

A Buddhist temple in the Henan province of east-central China. Built more than 1,500 years ago, popular legend says that the Shaolin Temple is the birthplace of kung fu.

Zen

Zen is a branch of Buddhism that emphasizes enlightenment and wisdom through direct experience, and especially through quiet meditation.

Above: A martial artist performs a tai chi form in a peaceful meadow.

INDEX